JawBreaker

Princeton Carter

To order additional copies of this book, contact:
Xlibris
844-714-8691
www.Xlibris.com
Orders@Xlibris.com

ISBN: Softcover   978-1-6641-5071-3
         EBook   978-1-6641-5072-0

Print information available on the last page

Rev. date: 01/11/2021

About the Author

Princeton Carter is a New Orleanian who recently graduated
from Wesleyan University. During the COVID-19 Pandemic, he
took the time to reflect over the traumatic racial events he has
witnessed and personally experienced. In an effort to heal and share
his truth, he began to write as a way to shed light on the issues
many black youth face as they grow up in today's America.

Foreword

Growing up in the South, Princeton frequented old country stores after Sunday church service. There, he noticed jars of jawbreakers in the back corner of the store. While watching kids take jar after jar home, he asked for a jar of his own. Today, these layered hard candies, full of different flavors and different colors remind him of the many layers of the black experience. The title of this book, "JawBreaker" reflects the oppression and brilliance that are attached to the legacy of black youth in America. Black youth have played pivotal roles in industrialization, activism, government, academia, athletics, and the very foundation of American society.

Through this book Princeton hopes to put black women in the spotlight. Black women, even within the black community, are frequently commodified and devalued due to the racist and misogynist beliefs that have been instilled into American society.

Black men should be advocates. Our pride should not be linked to our masculinity, our fragility, and the overall oppression of our own community. Too frequently black women and black transwomen are thrown to the wayside. The use of the description of "women" instead of "womxn" is favored because I believe if you identify as a woman, you are a woman, and therefore should be treated and identified as such.

All black women are essential in the fight for equality.

This book is written for black youth who feel they are alone in their plight against racism and misogyny. I have found that talking about the trauma I have compartmentalized has led to my healing. I hope it does the same for you. Especially during hard times like these, know that:

1) You are enough!
2) Your feelings are valid!

How to Read This Book

The best way to read this book is to start with the preface, then continue on with the piece below it.

Each piece is paired with an illustration that symbolizes images I pictured while writing each poem.

I hope you enjoy! Thanks for checking it out!

Table of Contents

Black Woman Affirmation

"I always win. It was never a tie.
We don't tie. We don't do overtime.
You're either behind me or behind me.
If you're in front of me, it's because I lapped you! I'm coming back"
- Chyna Rogers

Rest In Power To All The Black Women Whose Names
Have Been Erased From the History Books.

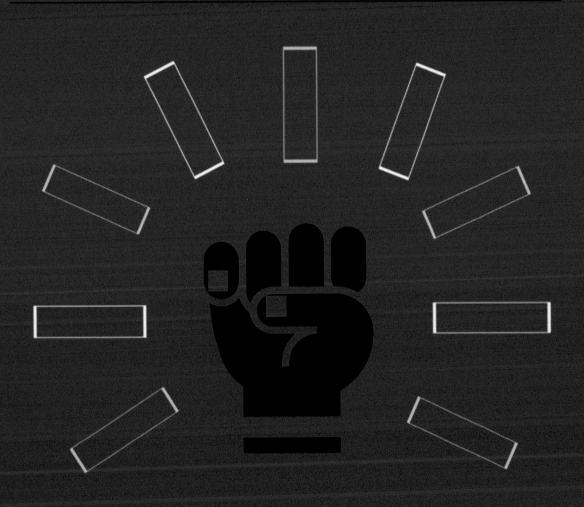

Black Women's Lives Matter

Breonna Taylor
Atatiana Jefferson

Sandra Bland

Bettie Jones
Tiara Thomas

Aura Rosser

Michelle Cusseaux
Janisha Fonville

Nuwnah Laroche

Natasha McKenna

Gabriella Nevarez
Tanisha Anderson

Yvette Smith

Black women are the heart and soul in the fight for equality.
They have sacrificed the most and received the least.

They deserve to be more than an afterthought.

Stripped of her humanity, stripped of her sanity, and yet-
She continues to win in a world that prayed on her downfall.

The Legacy

Exposure exposed her to an identity she had yet to become,
cultivated a community that cradled her conscience…..

only when it is convenient,

rooted in the unreciprocated love that holds us together,
skipping through the hate that tries to cripple her confidence,
battling for her autonomy while cinching to independence,
hypersexualized & disenfranchised,
undervalued & overlooked,
raped, robbed, tortured, and murdered,
royally resilient, rising from the remnants,
overqualified & underestimated,
persistent in her process & petty in her progress,
power in her presence, bomb in her bonnet,
courageously candid,
unapologetic & unforgettable,
indubitably incredible,
excluded from the constitution,
regal in her revolution,

She is a Black Woman.

Jesus is black. Judas worked for the feds.

_____

Trial of the Son

Courtesy is the curse of a Christian with a conscience,

Blood tastes better with tears running down my face,

The salt preserves the traumas I can never

repent from,

A snake without a nose can't taste the temptation,

Sweet slips of a tongue saturated in the memories I have yet to forget,

My voice was hushed before I parted my lips,

I tried to scream, but only bubbles came out,

Pickled the piccolo & paid the pied piper,

That note's kinda sharp,

Cherry filling leaking from the wholes I forgot to fill,

Violent stillness christens my corpse before my eulogy,

Please rise for the opening prayer,

He was betrayed by the state.

Criminalize our color and castrate our culture only
to exploit us for what they don't possess.

Generational Torture

watch the twinkle in their eyes dim as warm
stillness washes over plush virgin flesh,

a bullet is too quick. too loud. my palms. more intimate. more control.

Personal.

your grip on life is dependent upon mine.

a view from heaven from a seat in hell,

the heart rises as the air heavies,

i can hear the swastikas through the bed frame.

No love in this house.

i wasn't allowed in the house.

being able to inflict & feel pain simultaneously

playing victim from the seat of the executioner.

nothing like it.

loosening the grip on what's
tethered to humanity watch it dangle for the audience.

bravo! bravo! bravo!

They are more than family. They are the future.

Black women have created opportunities for all excluded minorities throughout the world. Their selfless acts of activism have been matched with their extraordinary ability to overcome the obstacles they face in their everyday lives. Their presence is activism, and their purpose is unwavering. The power of black women's presence in white dominated spaces, is seen in the tennis world. Venus and Serena Williams, in their early teens, joined the WTA tour. As they climbed their way up the rankings, they learned to dominate. During the Open Era of the WTA, the Williams sisters played each other for four consecutive grand slam finals. The dominance of both Venus and Serena, as black female athletes, created a ripple effect on the American tennis scene.

The Williams sisters faced many challenges of racism, gaslighting and sexism, during their rise to the top. Their presence in such a white dominated space, has created a ripple effect throughout the tennis world resulting in black women being at the forefront of American women's tennis.

A Legacy Inspired A Generation

There would be no Williams Sisters without Althea Gibson

There would be no Sloane Stevens without the Williams Sisters

There would be no Victoria Duval without the Williams Sisters

There would be no Taylor Townsend without the Williams Sisters

There would be no Naomi Osaka without the Williams Sisters

There would be no Coco Gauff without the Williams Sisters

The Legacy of the Williams Sisters has paved the way
for generations of courageous, unapologetic
young black tennis players.

Black women have a legacy of triumph that trumps
the challenges of the modern day.

Stole my heart and helped me look for it, gave me sandpaper instead of tissues. Tracks of my tears left scars on my dimples. You didn't save me, but you helped me accept that I don't need saving.

I'm glad you let me drown.

Cuffed to Colorism

Colonized complexions compromise the characters you pervert for expression.

Christened with contraception, feeding the fallacies for the approval of the king...or queen.

Your majesty!

eyelids covered in your calluses, keloiding as colorism reminds me why following bright ideas is your family tradition

I am the smudge.

My color conflicts with the comfort of your own home.

Didn't match the shades.

An almost perfect pic.

Almost.

mourning something that has been and never was.

Angry at the waiter for the entrée *you* ordered

Wasn't the first time you were mad it was darker than you thought…

not burned, I prefer.

Well Done.

You can only compromise so much until you compromise yourself.

Royal Witness

finding euphoria during my panic attacks

comfort only heightens the anxiety

vulnerability with each glance

shackled autonomy alluring to the free

jester to the queen who never acknowledged your lyrics

you both wear a mask beneath the makeup

lying for the audience. to the audience.

they cheer.

tears running down my chest

closest to the things we can smell but never taste

(just) powerful enough to witness what real power is.

Metal detectors before first period.

I Dismiss You

Would you like to share with the class?
You better not ask me to stand for the pledge,
While those who wear the flag turn high schoolers into h#sht#gs
If we "comply" we get 12 warning shots in our backs,
In our backpacks, In our snapbacks, in our snack packs,
minstrel facemasks across the faces of the targeted,
caught in the crossfire, caught in the fire's cross,

waiting for intervention?
protection?

Another unexcused absence.

No matter how old you are, you'll always be my baby.

Tamir & Emmett

boys will be boys

eenie meenie miney moe
shadrach, meshach, & abednego

the fire next time?
the fire last time.
our pain is in chains like they did our last names
lost in this cyclical sadistic *sanctuary* with no ID to ID home
drive-bys in cop cars from hidden clips revealing hidden slips
of the tongue,
another one. another one. another one.
watch the light leave his eyes, watch the life leave his eyes.
his name. his memory rinsed off the pavement of the block he once
called home,
diluted to distance the present from the past,
Rice from Till
both evicted from existence,
their lease on life has expired only to be gentrified
for the times we settled for progress.
Silently covering the pain. The pain silently uncovering you.

Pain is a loyal companion.

_____

For 526 seconds he drowned,
  The air compressed into his final sentence,
    I CAN'T BREATHE! I CAN'T BREATHE!
      They liked it. Shared it.
        Another lynching at the hands of the state,
          Squirming, Flinching, Pleading,
            He was suffocated, squeezed until he squealed,
              Trapped under the weight of the justice system,
                He screamed for help on Earth,
                  We watched. We heard, but didn't listen,
                    And as began to pass on,
                      as Man failed him,
                        He screamed to the heavens,
                          She was there on the steps to greet him,
Awaiting his arrival.

Black men. Check your privilege.

Get Your Mans

Get your mans!

Internalizing the generational traumas that have been glorified by your boys,

Hypermasculinity validating your predatory methods of talking to women

Gassing her appearance only to dismantle her value for your sexual pleasure

Disrespectfully dehumanizing a human being

Violating her vision.

Crucifying her character.

Groping her grace for the hopes of future sexual pleasure.

Disrespectful & Disgusting,

Mansplaining. Misogynoir. Microaggressions.

The neglect of blackwomen is self-destruction.

Objectifying & de-dignifying to confide in cyclical forgiveness,

You're only sorry for the consequences of your actions, not the weight of your recklessness

Shadows of the internalized hate projects into his perspectives.

black masculinity. black male fragility.

Accountability & Vulnerability. Support black women because they support

"Until they apologize specifically to Colin Kaepernick, or assign him to a team, I don't think that they will end up on the right side of history." – Malcolm Jenkins

---

#7

Color can touch but never mix,

    Checkered flag for the finish line,

Racin' the racist,

    Patient for me to perish so they can call in my replacement,

I'm expendable, my labor is not.

    My body is a commodity for America's economy,

Moving dreams threw the fields,

    Castrated if I kneel.

    1st Down.

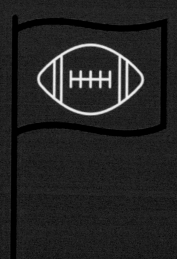

Black Mothers

my mom has a love that,

finds strength in vulnerability, comfortable with nudity from
days on the auction block --our modern-day draft night

my mom has a love that,

is unmatched and unwavering,

sobering as a siren & as forgiving as the future.

Heard through silence, speaking thousands of languages from facial
expressions alone.

She will not be silenced.

the soul of the revolution has rooted in her ascension,

Loves others before she loves herself

Selfishly selfless for the progression of her people

a mother when your moms away

powerfully patient and heroically humble as she,

shovels the liver down your pallet so
that you can have some bread pudding after

wipes your snot when you wallow in the pain from your first
breakup. (this seems random, why does this break)

fixes your bow tie before you strut across the graduation stage.

wipes the icing off your nose as she hands you
your second piece of birthday cake.

Pinches your ear as you whisper too loud during the
Sunday sermon

Screams when she finds out you're getting married
and later cries as we extend the family

The backbone of the black community

the engine. the fuel that pushes the envelope to
a better tomorrow at the expense of today.

When identity no longer exists, you are home.

Sunrise Mantra

Document the memories you fear you'll forget so that you
live every moment as if they're unforgettable.

Discomfort is the distance NOT the destination.

Sometimes I need more space than these walls can give me.

Understanding is a two-way street, be wary of one-way traffic.

Never plateau for your platform.

There's power in always being
present and never noticed.

Don't make permanent plans based
on temporary feelings.

The failures were lessons. Not let downs.

Just cause you found it unlocked,
doesn't mean it's open for u.

You are your words. Speak positively so that it will manifest.

Even in your longest chapters.

Morning Affirmation

I am beautifully, absolutely, unapologetically me, that is who I am supposed to be.

I'm a champion like Serena

I'm an icon like Eartha

I'm essential like Noname

I'm an activist like Fannie

I am beautifully, absolutely, unapologetically me, that is who I am supposed to be.

I'm powerful like Maxine

I'm a feminist like Bell

I'm as fearless as Audre

I'm as legendary as Angela

I am beautifully, absolutely, unapologetically me, that is who I am supposed to be.

I'm a boss like Michelle

I'm courageous like Assata

I'm unbreakable like Megan

I'm eternal like Maya

From the curls in my head to the souls of my feet, I am strong,

I am powerful, I am intelligent, I am me.

Printed in the United States
By Bookmasters